BACK INTO THE FIRE

POETRY
DAVID PITTS

NEWBERRY PARK

BACK INTO THE

POETRY
DAVID PITTS

FIRE

BACK INTO THE FIRE

NEWBERRY PARK

ISBN 0-9713954-0-3

TO:

"Where's poetry?"

The Thursday Night
Group.

SOUTH

NORTH

HYDRA

INTRODUCTION

When I put this book together the subject of the work fell loosely into two categories: poems inspired by the story-telling tradition of my grandmother, Muzzy, which are in the South section, and poems that are from a point of view impelled by my adult life which are in the North section. Poems written while I was living in Greece have also found their way into the book.

I spent my childhood in the port city of Jacksonville. My father worked for Texaco. The family: my father, mother, sister, grandmother, and I lived in a rented house on the company property. I had few friends and almost no concept of toys. I played among the real ships, trains, and trucks in my backyard.

When I was ten we moved across town. I had my own room and a smaller, quieter river in my backyard. There were kids in the neighborhood. My new toy was the violin.

After university I moved to the port city of Chicago where I spent most of my professional life creating advertising and teaching college.

When I was very young, and my mode of traveling was the Encyclopedia Britannica, I dreamed of living in Maine. Now at this end of my life, having traded the encyclopedia for a small sloop, and Lake Michigan for Casco Bay, I have set up shop in Maine.

SOUTH

"THAR SHE BLOWS"

High in the branches
                         of the chinaberry tree
               aloft in Pequod's crow's-nest
                             I scanned the horizon
       for the telltale spout.
            Searched the backyard dirt for
                       Moby Dick.
My sister stood watch
           ready to launch the harpoon boat
       listened for "thar she blows."
                Waited for me to scurry
                        down
         push the big tractor innertube
              out onto the waves.
     Leapt with me into the longboat
       to face the sea and
          The Great White Whale.
Pitchfork poised
         on my shoulder
    I stood at the bow while my sister
          pulled hard against the oars.
     Before us the whale
         surfaced.
   A long powerful heave
        buried
   the harpoon
           deep into the rising back.
"You kids get in here and wash up."

     We rowed back to the Pequod.

SAVING GRACE

For Joyce.

In the movies
 the girl always
 falls and sprains her ankle.
 Looks up from her
shredded-in-just-the-right-places
 blouse.
"I can't go on...I can't..."
 At the top of the hill
 he stops
 turns toward her.
 Will he go back?
 Or run
 for his life?

Joyce wanted to be
 saved.
 And Harry Christian was right there
 to save her.
He married her while I was off at school
 reading her love letters.
 Harry rescued her.
 Spared her the broken promises
 of this fugitive
 who wasn't
 coming back.

THE RETURN OF SAL CAMPOS

Sal's story.

A DosEquis bottle explodes
                                    at the edge of the bar.
                A shard swings from the torn label.
                        Flashes in my face.
Through the golden blur
                        I see his red balloon face
                                        burst.
                I taste spit and blood
                                    on the business end
                        of my fist.
He goes down on one knee
                convulsing like a gaffed
                                    dorado.
                A woman in sweat stained
                                flowers kneels over him.
                Curses me.
The blond with red bra straps
                        turns me back to the bar.
                My WildTurkey has melted
                                    in the heat.

RED TOUCHING YELLOW KILL A FELLOW

I remember
    I knelt.
        Dug in my knees
            toes.
          And like an old buccaneer
     returned to his treasure
        I smoothed away the sand
                grownover grass
         from the lid of the
               buried
        meter box.
My fingers
    tracked the edge.
        Found the lifting holes.
     I hesitated
        breathed cold adrenaline.
       Pictured the waiting
           treasure.
   Exhaled.
        Threw open the cover.
    Followed the Florida sun
      into the shallow well.
Blackeyed peas on stilts
        daddylonglegs
    goosestepped into grass.
   Asterisk size blackwidows
       climbed upon their mother's
          back.
    Scurried over her crimson
  timepiece.

Pillbugs, millipedes, centipedes
            silverfish
                        retreated from the light.
        With a handy stick
                        I plowed the damp bed
            until a spring of yellow rings
                        red and black bands
                                    uncoiled
            shed the debris of the treasure chest.
Rose erect from her
                        painted coils.
                                    Tasted my air.
            Whispered
                        "Red touching yellow
                                    kill a fellow."
My hand
        reckless of the warning
                                    touched
                                    a golden scale.
                        The snake recoiled.
        Crimson now lay beneath my
                                    finger.
            I lifted my hand.
                                    Another taste.
Red yellow black
            yellow red
                        slipped
            red yellow black yellow red
                        below the leaves.

SCOOPING

When I think about my dad
                I picture him as me
        in that I never saw him as a kid, of course.
                        So when I think about
                what he was like
        when I remember the stories
                        he told me over the years
                I picture me in the stories
                                doing the stuff he did.
My mom has pictures of him
                        as a young man
        when they were young together.
                But no real pictures of him
                                when he was a kid.
He had brothers.
                In fact, he referred to himself
                                and his brothers as
                The Pitts Boys.
                        As in, "Lock up your daughters
                The Pitts Boys are coming."
He had an old motorcycle
                        that was, of course, in those days
                (as when I myself had a motorcycle)
                                never ridden alone.
It was always he and one of his
                brothers
        flying around Williamson, Georgia
                                on that 1920's Indian.

I think of him
        but I picture myself and Steve
                        on my old 1950 Harley.
            Me and Steve
                    in his old pictures.
        Those brown and black
                            sepia pictures
                that actually look a lot like
                        Williamson, Georgia.
Red-brown clay dust rising
            from a red-brown road
        stretching across a red-brown field
                    trailing from behind a couple
                of red-brown boys on a motorcycle.
Actually
        he never really told me any
                        motorcycle stories.
            My father was a man
                        of few words.
                Very few words.
Instead, he would encapsulate
            a story into one scene
                    sort of like a movie trailer.
        You got the whole picture
                without having to hear the whole
                            story.

The motorcycle story
        went something like this:
     Steve and I would be bragging
           of our exploits on the Harley
      and my dad would walk over
            say something like
    "Yeah, we used to take corners
               so fast
          we'd scoop up dirt
      in our shirt pockets."
Now that's about the best
       motorcycle story I've ever heard
             before or since.
        So when I think of my dad
     sometimes I think of him
           on that motorcycle.
And I picture me and Steve
       flying around a corner
           scooping up dirt
  in our shirt pockets.

TYGER

Yesterday

                  a healthy

         full-grown

                         Siberian Tiger

           leapt to my shoulders.

      Licked my face.

A Florida carni

             had kept the animal

        in a small cage

                 barely fed it.

      "Two dollars a show.

             Poke it.

        See the vicious beast bare its teeth

                  and growl."

The State of Florida

                  confiscated the tiger.

        Now it lives with my friend, Raymond

                in a large cage

        with a fellow tiger.

        Thirty pounds of meat a day

               and Raymond.

Yesterday

                  a healthy

         full-grown

                         Siberian Tiger

           leapt on my shoulders.

      Licked my face.

THE BLIND PUPPETEER

The dishwasher was out again.
      And no money to replace it.
   Or have it repaired.
    "You'll need a phillips, a flatblade
      a crescent wrench and pliers."
My mother gathered the tools.
   Laid them out on the kitchen counter.

He'd been blind for seven years.
      But he'd fixed it twice before
   when he had sight.
       And like Geppeto
  my father guided my mother
    through the dismantling
  of the injured machine.
"Lay the parts out in order."
  Screws, bolts, gaskets, hose-clamps
       lined the kitchen floor.
   This time it was a broken belt.

The next time
   my father wasn't there.
  Like the machine
    a worn part had stopped him.
And no puppeteer
    to dismantle
  replace
     and reassemble.

SHARP KNIVES, MOTHERS, CAVEATS
AND BANANAS

Every morning I chop up a banana for my cereal.
                I hold the peeled fruit in my left hand
                        a paring knife
                in my right
        feed the banana between my thumb and
                                        the knife.
                        Scissorlike.
Maybe one morning in ten
        I'll hold the banana up straight
                slice it lengthwise
                twice tip to tip.
        Then crosscut
                into little pieshapes.
It was the way she did it.
        Before I was old enough to be entrusted
                        with a knife.
                "Keep the edge sharp.
        You'll never cut yourself with a sharp knife"
                        she'd say.
When I reach the butt-end of the banana
                        make the last cut
        I always test the blade.
        Scrape it against the flesh of my thumb.
                Give the edge a couple of passes
                        on the whetstone.
                Wipe the blade clean.
        "Don't leave any filings on the knife."

Place it back in the drawer
                edge down.

ALLIGATOR IN THE LIVING ROOM

First you need a sturdy rod.
> Ten feet is good.
> An old cane pole with the tip snapped off.
> > Some heavy wire.
Make a noose the size of your head.
> Slip the eye over the end of the pole.
> Wrap the wire tight.
A good flashlight.
> Rowboat.
> High tide.
> > New moon.

Moncrief River flowed behind our house.
> We slipped into the skiff.
> Pushed off.
> Steve rowed quietly
> > parallel to the shore.
I panned the shallows with the light.
> Two red eyes
> > glowed near a rotting piling.
> > Oars lifted.
I squeezed the flashlight against the pole.
> Leaned out over the bow.
> > Held the noose just above
the slate-still water.
> > "Stay up. Stay up."
The pole dipped.
> Jerked sideways.
> And up.
> > Hard.
> > "You got him."

Steve dropped an oar overboard.
          The flashlight rattled to the floorboards.
     I wheeled around.
                         Five feet of alligator
               in the air.
Flumped him into the rowboat.
          We lifted our bare feet.
     Afraid of losing toes.
                    In the blackness a tail slapped.
     Claws slashed.
                    Teeth snapped.
     Steve whooped and laughed.
                    Retrieved the oar.
     Rowed back to land.
I leapt
     squirming reptile in hand.
                    Ran for the light of the living room.
               "That's a beautiful animal.
     But I wouldn't put it on the carpet."
          My mother ran her finger
               over the dragon scales.
                         "Let it go soon.
               Before it dries out."

The alligator scrambled down the bank.
                    Swam out a few meters.
               Submerged.
     Steve and I turned.
               "Tomorrow, outrigger canoes."

29

SEX

They were black and white and the
nipples and pubic hair had been
air-brushed away.
Steve had found the nudist magazine
in his brother's room.
It was the best we could do at the time.
Nineteen forty-eight.
Ten years before Playboy.
We were nine.
Slowly turning the pages, we savored
each photograph.
Naked girls playing volleyball.
Beachball.
After we'd paged through the magazine
two, three times
we folded it
and buried it in a secret hole
under a marked brick in the walk.

I am standing on those bricks now.
The house is gone.
The yard looks small.
And I wonder...
not if the pictures are still there
but under which brick.

ESCAPE

My father's Texas Oil Company.
    The redneck jokes in the warehouse.
My mother's two-chair beauty shop.
   The laid-in-place-but-never-glued-down
            linoleum.
At seventeen I left Jacksonville
     and most of me has never
   looked back.
I've gone back.
    Even smiled at the redneck jokes.
      Driven past the old
   beauty shop.
   Listened to Billy Hill tell how I used play
      with the curling irons
    on that shop floor.
But like any escaped convict
   I keep my distance.
    Move carefully amongst the crowd.
My mother feels it.
   Asks why I can't "just be more like
       your sister...
    move on back down here
   close to the family?"
As I drive back to the airport
   a prison roadgang is working
      the median.
     A kid about the age of escape
   looks up
      catches my eye.
I smile
   gesture in the direction
     of the airport.

SOFTBALL

My grandmother used to say
                         "Many are called.
              But few are chosen."
It was always the same.
                         "Saturday, we want everybody
          to come out for softball."
                    But sure as I'd be there
                         neither side would choose me.
                              And I was a good hitter
          as good as anybody.
                    To be honest... fielding
                         was another matter.
I could pitch too.
                              Didn't seem to matter.
              There were always the guys
                    who just had the positions.
          You know.
                    J.E. will pitch.
              Scott will play First.
                         (Scott had one of those
          right-hand-first-baseman's-gloves.)
So on it went.
          As if worked out in some non-existent
                                   previous meeting.
Of course
          if one of the chosen few didn't show up
                         I could
              maybe
          if there was no one
                              else
                    bat last and play right-field.

And even though I would
    consistently
        drive-in one of the chosen few
    or get stranded out on second
        by the chosen few
    the next week
        it would be the same thing
        all over again.
My grandmother is dead now.
    Up there in that sandlot in the sky.
    And I sure hope she's got one of those
        right-hand-first-baseman's gloves.
        "Many are called.
    But few are chosen."

DEFINITION

At ten I picked up the violin.
           Too late for virtuosity.
                But for a decade it defined
                  my life.
At twenty-two
          on an otherwise forgettable
       September afternoon
              I put it down.
                  And for three decades
        some bit of definition
            lies with that lost violin.

MAYPORT

Saturday would come
                         and again seduce me
           to the beach.
To that last rock
       at the end of the jetty
                 where I would run-stumble
       fly-leap
    along foamy rip-rap.
                Scratch and climb
                       another mile
            to my rock.
Then glued against the waves
          sit and stare across the harbor
                 at the aircraft carriers
      moored in the basin.

When the Saratoga steamed past
              my personal reviewing stand
        crispy-white sailors
                 at parade rest
     belied the war that I knew only
             as a great grey ship
       that sailed with shrimpers
       and sailboats
            on Florida Saturdays.

BACK INTO THE FIRE

When I was a kid
                    seven, eight, nine
          and I burned my hand
     or anything else
                         for that matter
               my mother
          would have me
                    hold the burned
     fingers, elbow, knuckles
                         back in the fire.

She said the fire
               would draw out the pain.
     I didn't believe it
                    anymore then than I do now.
                         But I did it for her.
          She believed it.
     And she was right about most things.
                    Most of the time.

So back into the fire
               would go my hand.
                              And maybe
     just maybe it would work this time.
               Maybe last time
                         I hadn't held it in
               long enough.

I'm older now.

              Forty-seven, eight, nine
     and I've been burned

                    once again.
        And again I'm going to reach
           back into the fire.
Knowing, of course, that it doesn't work.
        Knowing it's just going to be
          painful.
             But if I do nothing.
    Let the pain heal.
        The fire die.

Maybe

       if I held it in the fire
   longer?

SEPTEMBER DRAGONS

We'd seen it on TV.
                        The Ed Sullivan Show.
        I cut a short length of garden hose.
                Slid it down into the tank
    of my dad's Chevrolet.
                        Leaned over
        sucked up a mouthful.
                Ran into the dark of the side yard.

Steve struck a match
                on his thumbnail.
                        Held it just in front of my lips.
        I pushed his hand back
                        as the flame
                singed the hairs on my nose
        then exhaled spit and gasoline
                                over the match.
                A ball of orange and blue flame
    rolled and rose in the cool twilight.

"Your turn."

                Steve blew out the match.
        Ran back to the car.

MISSING

A little fellow
              in a photograph
          sits at the piano
                      his precious violin
              in his hands.
A look of
            commitment
                   anticipation
             peace
                    in his face.
David nine years old
          on the back of the picture.

At breakfast
                my milk carton asks
      if I've seen another child.
                   But I'd like to find
        that little fellow
             in my photograph.

It won't matter
                that he doesn't still play
      the violin.

CHECKING OUT

I've only a carton of icecream
        three bananas
  skim milk
     and a box of Grapenuts.
Her handbasket looks quick
      so I pull in
   behind her.
  Milk, eggs, oranges
       a package of chicken breasts
         pita bread
    and three cans of tomato paste
  slide over the magic scanner.
Arabic numbers flash
   and beep.
       Paper numbers
  roll up in front of her.
    The scale under the oranges shows
       one-point-seven pounds.
"That'll be twelve-eighty."
       She reaches for her purse.
    Unsnaps the flap.
       Unzips the pouch.
  Digs...
     Coupons
   wrapped with a rubber band
        two lipsticks
    address book
  check book
   pack of Marlboros
      two tampons
     bottle of Advil
       her wallet.

She touches a twenty,
          a ten, "Let's see now, five...six...
                    seven...eight...nine...
     was that twelve-eighty?"
"Yes maam...
          Twelve-eighty, maam."
                    "Oh..." and a little smile.
"Eleven...twelve...
          twenty-five...fifty...sixty...
                    seventy...seventy-five...
     seventy-six...seventy-seven...
                              seventy-eight..."
She looks at the change
                    disapprovingly
          offers a ten and three ones.
The cashier rings me up
                    and I squeeze by
                              as she
          replaces the clutter
                    of her purse.
"Can you get by?" she asks politely.
          The question is too complicated
     to ponder
                    and my icecream is melting.

SKIPPING STONES

One – two – three

$\qquad\qquad\qquad$ four

$\qquad\qquad$ five – six – seven – eight

$\qquad\qquad\qquad\qquad$ nine.

Choose a good stone.

$\qquad\qquad\qquad$ Flat

$\qquad\qquad\qquad\qquad\qquad$ round

$\qquad\qquad$ no sharp edges to catch

$\qquad\qquad\qquad\qquad$ the wind

$\qquad\qquad\qquad$ or the surface.

$\qquad$ A little weight

$\qquad\qquad\qquad$ for momentum.

$\qquad\qquad$ Silver dollar size.

Hold it level

$\qquad\qquad\qquad$ on the third finger.

$\qquad$ Thumb on top of

$\qquad\qquad\qquad\qquad$ the stone.

$\qquad\qquad$ Index finger

$\qquad\qquad\qquad$ firm

$\qquad\qquad$ against the forward edge.

$\qquad$ As if you were going to flip

$\qquad\qquad\qquad\qquad$ heads or tails.

Throw sidearm.

                                     Low.

                    Off the right foot.

                                              Follow through.

                              Aim parallel to the surface.

          Let gravity bring it down

                            soft and flat.

No wind is best.

                        A shore breeze OK

                            flattens the sea.

Competition

                    record-keeping

              not required.

Just you

          a mile or so

                    of smooth glacial remnants.

              Cumulonimbus.

                        A Prussian sky.

Technique.

THE CLOTHES HAMPER

In the upstairs bathroom.
                         The only bathroom
            in that old Victorian house where
                                    I was born
                         was a hamper.
            Wicker.
                         White.
            With a wooden lid.
It stood against the wall just to the right
                                    as you walked in.
                         Right across
            from the tub and the toilet.
                         It was a rainy February day.
            My sister, Page
Steve from down the street
            and I were playing hide-and-go-seek.
                                    It was my turn.
            We'd worn out all the good places.
            Except, maybe (if I could get into the thing)
                         the hamper.
I was a skinny kid.
            It ended up being a lot easier
            than I thought.
                         The getting in part.
            Lying there
back-down on the damp towels
                         knees in my face
                         I realized how well I could see
            through the screen of wicker.

The bathroom door closed.
                    And locked.
        Blood pulsed in my cramped knees.
                          My dad's sister, Evelyn
                (staying with us overnight
                        on her way up to Atlanta)
            was bending over the tub.
                                Running water.
In one second
            the whole story
        played in my head:
                    I pop open the lid
                    of the hamper.
                          Announce to Aunt Evelyn
                that I'm just playing hide-and-go-whatever
                and spend the rest of my life
                          a sexual pervert.
I kept very still.
                    Shortened my breaths.
            Aunt Evelyn sat on the lid of the toilet.
                          Pushed off her shoes.
        Unsnapped her hose from the garter belt.
                Rolled down her stockings.
"Oh my God.
            She's going to put them in the hamper."
        She placed them neatly
                        on the lid.
                Took off her skirt.
                            Blouse.

She then reached around with both hands
                              unsnapped her brassiere.
                    Rolled her shoulders forward
                    let the brassiere slide down her arms
                                        into her hands.
                    Bent over the hamper and placed it
                              with the her other things.
They were perfect.
                    A couple of the boys at school
                                        with older sisters
                              had seen breasts.
And we'd all seen our mother's.
                              But these were right there.
                                        I watched them.
          Washed.
                    Rinsed.
                         Patted dry.
After Aunt Evelyn left the bathroom
                    I rocked over the hamper.
                    Hurried downstairs.
                              Page and Steve
          were playing rummy in front of
                                        the fireplace.
                         "No fair hidin' outside, Dirtbag."
I wanted to tell Steve.
                    I didn't.
          Ever.

GLASS EYES

When I was five or six
                    my mother took me to the
               Jacksonville Public Library.
In a small cyclorama
          a Florida panther
                         in the underbrush
                                    of a Live Oak
               reared on his hindlegs
                              teeth bared
                    front claws threatening.
He'd been there a very long time.
          I reached over the rail and touched him.
                         His body cavity was hollow.
               His eyes glass.

Years and miles
          from that Florida panther
                         I have stood too long
               among plaster trees
                         papier maché undergrowth.
I touch the hollowness in
                         my
                                    chest.

47

DESIRE

The car was not air-conditioned.
                              Maureen had unbuttoned
              every button
                         down the front of her sundress.
She drove with her left hand
                         and with her right
              rubbed a cold dripping coke
                                   across her breast.
"Wanna sip?"
              She held out the big red and white cup.

State road nine ran through the
                              Florida half
              of the Okeefanokee.
"Pull over."
                         She braked hard.
       Tires skidded over longleaf pine needles.
I swung out of the passenger side.
                         Ran back sixty or seventy yards.
       Maureen closed a few buttons.
                              Walked toward me.

Four feet from the road an
                         Eastern Diamondback
              had moved out of the palmettos.
                    Slid resolute along the shoulder.
I stood in the path of the large snake.
                         She paused.
              Drew back her head.
                              Resumed her glide.

I stepped away.
My bluff called.
The snake moved toward the shelter
of the palmettos.
Fearful of losing her to the forest
I again stepped into her path.
Her head moved close to my foot.

Do it.
The adrenaline commanded.
My hand grabbed the snake just behind the head.
Her body coiled
around my arm and neck
took hold of me with unanticipated
power.
Was she strong enough
to pull me to her?
Sink her fangs into my flesh?
I pulled her head close to mine.
Bared my teeth.
Brought her closer.
Breathed across her nostrils.

Slowly, knowing what I wanted
the snake dropped her jaw.
Rolled out the glistening fangs.
At the tip of each hung
an amber drop of venom.
I wanted to feel that poison
run through my veins.
Desire pushed up the core of my body.

Maureen, buttons in unrelated buttonholes
                    circled with the Nikon.
        "Put it down before it bites."
                    A drop of venom fell
            onto the back of my hand.
I wanted to taste it.
                Rub it into my skin.
        But wiped it cautiously onto my jeans.
                        Maureen was right.
                I kneeled.
        Laid coil after coil onto warm sand.
                Released the head.
                            Jumped away.

The snake lay still a moment.
                Slipped back into the palmettos.

VIRTUOSITY

The closest
        I ever came to greatness
                        on the violin
                was the time
I shyly reached over
        and plucked the D string
                        of Fritz Kreisler's
Stradivarius.

DAYDREAMS

Concerto
The maestro pushes past allegro vivace.

                   I answer in flying staccato.

          Soar in flying staccato.

    The orchestra is seduced.

          A fire sweeps

               across the audience.

         I answer in pyrotecnic tempo.

Night Landing
It's a black dot

        on a blacker sea.

     But the white spray defines the rolling

                   pitching deck.

       Rain pours through the three

           holes in the canopy.

     Washes the three matching

           holes in my flight jacket.

I turn final.

     Drop the gear and crab in.

          The stick is slick with spray

      and blood.

Everything goes black

    as I pick up the hook.

Touché
I can just see his eyes
                    behind the mask.
          They're riveted on mine.
                         Keep them there.
A rattlesnake strikes
               from my left foot
          to my right hand.
                         Touché!
                    He never saw my hand move.
Next time I'll give it away.
               Then...
                         Degagé!

HICKORY TREE STORIES

Actually it got him killed.
                              "How's that?"
                    Well let me tell you.
He was lying there on the cool cement
                                        of the carport.
                Out of the direct sun
                            but in the breeze.
                                In the breeze
                    blowing across the cool cement floor
                            of the carport.
But she sat
        perched in the sun.
                        Perched and looking at him
                with that look
                            only a Blue Jay
            in the hot summer sun
                            can look at a lazy cat
                    lying on the cool cement
                                of the carport.
But a look was not enough.
                    There were young Blue Jays.
                Her young Blue Jays.
                                        So a look
                    was not enough.
A fly-through was in order.
                    A fly through the carport
                                just under the eaves.
            Just over the cat
                        full speed.

He would tell stories about that day.
                              About the day he leapt
                        five feet into the air.
              Snatched that Blue Jay right out of the sky.
Tell stories out back
                  under the hickory tree
            how he pulled that Blue Jay
                              right out of the sky.

"But you said it killed him."
              I did say that, didn't I.
            Yes, on another summer day high up in that
                              hickory tree
                        he tried it again.
              Tried to grab another Blue Jay
                              out of the air.
Now I wouldn't say he was
                        unsuccessful.
            He did catch the Blue Jay.
                  But the fall to the driveway
            did him in.
Catching Blue Jays one-handed
                        did him in.

1946

The breakfast table was green
                        the color of 55 gallon drums of
           Texaco Havoline 10W-30.
Our rented house was one of two
                            on the Texas Company property.
              The porch floorboards
        and the house trim
                    were the same green.
My father made the table
                  when I was two.
              It sat in the kitchen
                          against the south wall.
Some mornings there would be
                a brand new box
           of Nabisco Shredded Wheat.
                            Unopened.
Red, white, and blue.
                The blue on the purple side.
         The cardboard a sort-of industrial
                      brownish-gray-white.
The biscuits were pillow-shaped
                    in two layers
           separated by a card.
                    This was before spoon-size.
I liked shredded wheat
                but I really liked
                      the cards.
        The subject of this day's card was:
                "How to build a compass."

I hurried through my cereal
                    collecting mentally
          the items needed:
                              magnet
                              shallow dish
                              cork
                              sewing needle
                              sheet of paper
                              ruler
                              pencil or pen
                    Easy stuff.
My mother cleared the table.
                    I gathered the necessary items.
          My father read aloud the instructions.
               A paragraph about Magnetic North.
                    True North.

The compass sat on the green table
                    for a few days
          until my mother washed the dish
          and put the needle
                              back
               into her sewing basket.
In the next days I hurried through
                    the shredded wheat.
          Anticipating the next box
                    and a new card.

ROCHESTER
Stephanie's story.

When I was a little girl
                    five or six
          or even sixteen...

                                        on Saturdays
                    my mother and I
                              would take the PACE bus
          to the city.
When we got to our stop
                    and were standing on that yellow stripe
          that everybody stands on
                              when they are getting ready
          to get off the bus
Mr. Abernathy
                    the bus driver
          would always look over at me and say
                              "Rochester."
At first I would smile
                    as if it meant something nice...
          take my mother's hand
                              and be off.
But after a while
                    years actually
                              it started to annoy me.
                    "Rochester?"
          Why would he say that to me?
The name of the bus was THE LOOP EXPRESS.
                    My mother's name is BERTHA.
          My name is STEPHANIE.
Oh, I know, you're way ahead of me.
                              You're thinking he's calling out
                                        the stops.
          And for a long time I too believed that.

We did always get off the bus
at Ohio and Michigan.
But neither of those words sounds like
"Rochester."
Maybe it was the name of a store
or a section of town.
Like Streeterville or Homewood.
But it wasn't.
It was just Ohio and Michigan.
Why was he saying this to me?
Maybe it was his name.
"That's it.
His name is Rochester.
Like the guy on the Jack Benny show."
The next time
while my mother was putting the fare
in the fare box
I sucked up all my nerve and squeaked
"Good morning, Rochester."
"Good morning to you too, Miss..."
For a second the mystery was over.
I felt proud and life had meaning again.
"It's Howard, Miss, Howard Abernathy."
I slung into my seat.
Eventually the bus arrived at our stop.
I made no eye contact with Mr. Abernathy.
As surely as the sound of the airbrake
"RO-CHE-STER."
"Yes, dear," said my mother
"WATCH-YOUR-STEP."

SHARKS' TEETH

For Tony - age nine.

They say
        that lions are better
                fit
           for biting
                than for being
                    bit.
But I think
        it's far more
                true
           of our friend the shark
                Don't you?
If a lion breaks a
        tooth
      on a bone or on a
                hoof
           does another one grow
                back
           right away to fill the
                    slack?
The shark
        (on the other paw)
           has inside that fearsome
                jaw
           rows of teeth to shame
                    a feline
      loose a few
        they're back in no time.
The lion's got no leg
        to stand on
           when eating with reckless
                abandon.

Lions eat stuff like
            wildebeest
        whereas sharks will often feast
                    on fish and boats
            seals and skates
                    tourists, turtles
                        and license plates.
So when it comes to dental
                    danger
            give the lion to Stewart
                            Granger.
For by far
        it's my belief
                    the shark deserves
            the prize for
                    teeth.

FIRST NUDE

Class began at eleven forty-five.
                                        I walked in
                    with the always-on-time group.
She slipped in just ahead of the instructor.
                              Stepped onto the platform.
             Removed the teal green robe.
                    Pushed off the black flats.
Sat back into an unpainted wicker arm chair.
             Mr. Hagenseeker whispered and gestured.
                                 She assumed her pose:
                    Hips deep into the chair.
                    Back almost straight.
                    Arms following the lines of the chair.
                    Left foot flat on the floor.
                    Right leg over the chair arm.
I had just put a new sized canvas onto my easel
                              was tightening the wing-nuts
             that hold the canvas frame in place
                    when Mr. Hagenseeker stepped away
                              from our new model.
             Bernini had stepped away from Venus.
I don't know how long I had been staring.
                              But she smiled, just a small
                    not-to-break-the-pose smile
                                        which I read as
             "I have never been naked before
                              but I'm doing this just for you."
I was torn between staring and painting.
                    Soon someone, her mother, husband
             or the police would surely come
                              and throw a blanket over her.

Her face was paradisaic.
Those lips that had just smiled
were back in place
forming an ionic capital
under her Hellenic nose.
And her breasts.
My grandmother would cook biscuits
on Sundays.
They would pop up straight out of the tin.
Toasty tan on the top.
Firm and white on the sides and bottom.
I admit I spent a long time studying her breasts.
But I gave ample attention
to every inch of her form.
For minutes
I compared the shape of the inside of her navel
to the opening in her left ear.
The little hairs on the side of her neck
to the puff of pubic hair
resting on the raw unpainted wicker.
Suddenly she rose from her pose.
Slipped back into the teal green robe.
Pushed her feet into the black flats.
Stepped down from the platform.
More whispers and gestures from Mr. Hagenseeker
and she was gone.
"Miss Davenport will only be with us this week...
hope you all got a good start."
I looked at my canvas.
The wing-nuts were still loose.

MUSICAL CHAIRS

I am standing
                    over by the box office window.
          Out of the way
                    but in view of the man behind the cage.
                              It's just after seven-fifty.

My father bought it for me
                    when I was nine.
          Paulus Music Shop on Adams.
                              It wasn't a Strad
                                        or a Guarnieri.
                    But a good violin.
          First-chair, second-violin in school.
          Fifth row, first-violin in college.
                    Same spot in the hometown orchestra.

It was in the fall.
                    I was twenty.
          Maybe Sandra
                    my girlfriend and accompanist
          had run off and married a cop.
                              Or I was married
                    with a kid.
          Maybe I was moving to Chicago.

I cleaned the rosin from the fingerboard.
Loosened the strings
and the hair of the bow.
Laid the violin in the case.
Eased its neck into its green felt cradle.
Snapped the bow into place in the lid.
Closed the case.

"I've taken up the fiddle
would you like to see it?"
It was fall again.
I was fifty.
She popped open the case.
Jerked out a violin.
"Neat, huh, you wanna hold it?"
I hesitated.
Placed it under my chin
tightened the hair on the bow.
Tuned, handed back her violin.

"Sir."
The man behind the bars looks squarely at me.
"I have a seat."
I walk forward.
Slide my VISA card.
"Eighth row, right in the center.
A very good seat."

I think I gave it to my sister.
        Or my girlfriend's older brother had a kid
               taking lessons.
      I was busy getting away
                from Jacksonville.
The geeky guy with the classical records
     and the high-school letter
                 in orchestra.

It is a good seat.
          Just not the one I had
    when I was twenty.

PINE SNAKE

The late morning stones were warm
                                    against my back.
                That warmth and the
                                    rough stones
        brought her
                    to my wall.
Her head
                like new brocade
                        had cast off its old skin
            which clung like a ruffled collar
                                    to her back.
As she moved
                        flints peeled back more.
                Revealed a gleaming bolt
                            rolled out in front of me.
She slipped over the wall.
                Dragged her translucent remnant.
        I, wanting to help
                            to possess
                reached after her.
                    A bit of weightless film
        broke off in my fingers.
I sat for awhile.
                Examined the small cameo of scales
                        that matched the silver ribbon
            on the forest floor.

NORTH

LATINICUS SOMETHING-OR-OTHER

At first
                    I didn't notice.
          Three green stems.
I moved my head
                    a little to the left.
          Isolated one against the white wall
                                        of a house.
The petals were the exact color of the
                                        sea behind them.
          I rocked my head
     back to the right.
                    The flowers disappeared.

Halfway up the walk
          the Paros sun had stopped me.
     I sat with my groceries.
                    Squinted out over Naousa Bay.
My wife informed me
          they were:
     Latinicus Something-Or-Other.
                              Obviously
          named by someone who
                    didn't at all understand
          the nature
                    of the
     Flowers That Disappear Into the Sea.

THE FOX AND THE PHOTOGRAPHER

He came to photograph
                    wildlife.
        And he came

                    prepared.
        With his three-hundred millimeter lens
                                wife
                    and two young sons.
        They would go deep
                        into the forest.
            And maybe
                if they were very very

                            quiet.
                    And very very
                            still
                they might see...
The fox
        standing in a handicap parking space
                            watched
            the volvo station wagon
                    pull into the parking area.
        Watched the little troupe
                        disembark.
                Stood quietly
                    as the father snapped on
        the zoom lens.
                    Loaded the film.
                        Packed the camera case.
                Adjusted the tripod.

Then, as if satisfied with their
                                    readiness
                                            and preparation
                the fox
                        unnoticed and unstirred
                                trotted across the highway.
Bounded off
            into the woods.

AFTER BEAUTY

When I was beautiful
　　　　I loved beauty.
　　　Saw only beauty around me.
　　　　　　The Tiger taught me stealth.
　　　The Eagle gave me vision.
　　　　　　　From the Wolf
　　　　I learned fraternity.
　I watched the Fer de Lance.
　　　　　Sought patience and humility.
　　　　　　　Feared not the serpent
　　　only my carelessness.

Now I am ugly
　　　　and hate beauty.
　　　See only ugliness around me.
　　　　　　The Tiger shows me I am weak
　　　　　　　　and clumsy.
　　　To the Eagle
　　　　　　I am blind.
　The Wolf rears its young
　　　　and I long for my children.
　　　I stumble through the forest
　　　　　　　in fear
　　　　of the Fer de Lance.

SEPARATED

My wife has become an estranged sister.
My lover nonchalant.
Suggests I not sleep over.
My friends are spending the week in Michigan.
Or did the voicemail say
Saint Thomas?
Tomorrow my watch will say it is June.
But it has rained for eight days.
Fog has drawn the color from the city.
And the wind off the lake
dresses me for March.
A colleague tells me my writing has no
feeling to it.
She is right.
My home is like a hotel room.
Numb fingers make polyester
of my damask couch.
I have forgotten where we keep
the tablespoons.
The waitress at the diner asks if I want my eggs
in a cup.
Everything is cardboard and chalk.
I carry my toothbrush and comb
in my pants pocket.

UNDERSTUDY

It was not I that lingered
                 on the side of the bed
                     this morning.
Watched you toss your dress
           over your head.
        Saw it smooth over those small
                   delicate breasts.
I did not rise
         to secure that little
              top button.
       Feel your fingers
           reach back to guide
                mine.
I did not take your narrow shoulders
          in my hands.
          Push my face into the nape
            of your neck.
       Into that lemon hair.
           Taste the memory
     of last night.
I did not pull your straight back
          to my chest.
      Rest my chin on the crown
         of your mysterious head.
It was not I.

CANDIDE

You never learned to swim.
                    No big deal.
          We said.
You bought the red one-piece.
                    I swam with Lanie.
                         "Here's your towel.
          Again tomorrow?
                              Noon?
                    You looked good today."

You never learned to ski.
                    Not important.
          We agreed.
You did the galleries.
                    I skied with Annette.
                         "One more run?
          Then down to Tiehack?
                              Lunch?
                    You looked good today."

You never learned to sail.
                    Sat in the cockpit.
          On fair days.
Smooth seas.
                    I sailed with Lorra.
                         "Those are humpbacks.
          A little ease on the jib.
                    Provincetown tomorrow.
                         You look good tonight."

DACHAU

Dead.
    White.
                A girl eighteen.
       Nineteen.
            Schoolgirl.
                 Clerk.
        Bean shoot
           grown in darkness.

Dead.
    White.
       Light
           on a school auditorium screen.
Nineteen forty-eight.
       My nine year old eyes
              wide.

Dead.
    White.
       Snow.
The sleeping fairy
         slides naked
           down the embankment.
       Stick pile of arms
              legs.
       Grass stalks
         under a rock.
            Schoolgirls.
             Clerks.

SPRING

April taps its shoulder
                      and the earth
              head-down
                                    hunched
          collar-up against winter
                                              turns
                  leans into the light.

RUNNING WITH SCISSORS

The world is a dangerous place.
And for my money
baby
that's just the way I like it.
To serve and protect:
Well, I don't want to be protected.
Can't be anyway.
Somebody wants to put a little LSD
in my Metamucil
who's gonna stop 'em?
You think some law
against fiber tampering
will do the trick?
Law and Order:
Order I like.
We've just gotten around to believing
if we make a law against anything
and everything
that can possibility hurt us
we'll be safe.
Example:
Some farmer's pig
roots his way under the fence
runs into town
bites a nine-year-old.
Do we shoot the pig?
Make a new law:
Mandatory adequate confinement
of hydrophobic swine.

Or do we just laugh.
Give a fudge soda to the catcher of the pig
and the nine-year-old
who can pull up his pants in school
show his scar.
Let's take down the fences
around our swimming pools.
Hold a spider.
Pick up a snake.
Go to Turkey.
Fish next to a bear in a mountain stream.
Touch a bat.

LIGHTLY

A young couple
            sit at the table next to me.
        He is in love.
                        And she likes him.
Her hands lie flat on the table.
                                    As he talks
                        he lightly touches
            the top of her hands
                        with the tips of his fingers.

He would trade his whole life for her
                    to lightly touch the top of his
                                        hands.
But she has never touched
                the top of hands lightly.
            She has never had to.

He is in love.
            And she likes him.

SUVA VITI LEVU

Suva is the capital of Figi on the island of Viti Levu.

VOICE 1.	VOICE 2.
Naked island girls	Black bra
half hidden behind	half hidden beneath
shore palms	orange tanktop
giggle	begs cigarettes
as our landing boats	as our dingy
surf	noses
onto spread tablecloth	sludgefoam onto
white	toxic
beach.	beach.

ENGRAM

Cats have sharp claws
                    and big teeth
          and we don't like that.
When they bite us
     it hurts.
                    And we curse God
                    for making them like that.
Suck our bloody finger
                    and wonder
          why she couldn't have
                    just bought a dog.

RIVER

I walked beside a river
                    and came upon a tiger
            drinking.
                        I stopped and drank.
The tiger
                seeing me
                    finished his drink.
        Returned to the forest.

"What a wonderful thing I have seen
                        drinking
        at the edge of the river."

DIVORCE

Is all that we see or seem, but a dream within a dream? EAP

Is life a movie?
                Little parts that have their own
      brief time?
                        Their own beginning
            middle
            end?
Was that Saki story we?
            I see you now and I say
      "Hello."
                    You say, "Hello."
          You're very nice.
        As if we'd gone to the movie
                  together.
Sometimes we even mention
        the movie.
                Talk about some of the scenes:
      That Night off Sambro Light
          The House in Wilmette.
              As if it were some old classic.
      Actors we'd heard of
         but don't really remember.
                Young on screen.
          Dead in real life.
Was it good enough to see again?
           Would we want to see it together?
        Or would it be just as well
             to see with someone
                    else?

SHE

A Maypole.
        Rigid.
    Constant.
                 Axis to my gyre windings.
Arms radiant.
        Tether ribbons.
    Taut.
              Unseverable.
Each orbit
      blazing
    transplendent.
              Force centripetal.

THE PROXY

I am pondering her Chardonnay words.
Staring
into my Sam Adams.
Thoughts roll around the rim of my glass.
Collected, I look up.
The words are on my tongue.
But a Cyrano man on the radio
puts his finger to my lips
and sings.
She smiles approvingly.
Once more
I twist my tongue around a concept.
When I am ready
again
he sings to her.
"Yes," she smiles.
I stare deep into the foamy clouds.
My wits and courage surface.
I breathe deep.
Lean forward.
Again, the Tin Pan Alley man sings.
She bites her lip.
Rolls the lyric over in her head.
Nods to the beat of the music.

ONE VERSION

It all started when
               nothingness blew up
          and created
                    hydrogen
                         which blew up
               and created
                    Chopin.

DIVORCE II

Well meaning friends
                each a shark from the circling pack
       dart in
                bite at my resolve.

NATALIE AND THE STORM PETREL

Natalie slipped from her mother's cabin
                    climbed to the upper deck
        stepped once
                    "Oh, my"
                        twice
            upon the lace trim of her nightgown.
    Leaned, chin and elbows on the teak rail.
                    Stared out over the still and
                        endless
            mooney-greeny-black.

A storm petrel
            displaced by the calm
    lighted at her left elbow.
                "How did you get all the way out here?
                    You're so small
        and you have such tiny wings?"

Natalie held out her arms
                let her nightgown fill
                        with the light breeze
                created by the moving ship
                            turned slowly
        ran back to her mother's cabin.

ARTIFICIAL HORIZON

Once a man stood at the edge of the sea.
                    Gazed out to the horizon.
          Watched the ships rise and sink.
                         And by this deduced
                the spherical nature
                              of our planet.
I stand at the end
            of and old pier.
        Stare out to the sea.
                   Fearing that the world
                                is round.
To me all of tomorrow
                is just over a horizon
            that does not
      curve downward
                and come up in my backyard.
I believe in a horizon that dips
                      just enough
             to hide the known world
         then rises up and widens
                              infinitely
      to accommodate my wildest
                    and most preposterous
           fantasy.

UN BEL DI

The problem is
                Pinkerton always shows up
        around dinner time
                   to claim
              what is "rightfully"
                             his.
And the only thing that keeps me
         from doing the harakiri
                       number
               is
            we all sing again
    tomorrow.

93

PHOTOREALISM

In the movie
              Dana Andrews falls in love
       with a picture
                     of Gene Tierney
                            who is dead
              but isn't really
       who comes back
                     and falls in love
              with him.

Now I am wondering.
                     Is this a good thing
       she falling in love with him
                     just because he's gone
              to all this trouble
                            to fall in love
       with her
                     picture?

BALBO AND WABASH

The el platform caught most
                of that October rain.
            But the wind drove me
                        into a shallow doorway.

SHILLER'S HOUSE OF MUSIC

I glanced west, hoping for a bus.
                        then leaned back
            against the cool glass door.
                A woman
                        in a chrome yellow slicker
            swooped into the tiny alcove.
                    An encased viola in one hand.
                            Sodden umbrella in the other.
I reached to help with the door.
                    She, ignoring my gesture
            elbowed her way through
                        and my fingers
                trailed
            across her wet plastic.
Again I leaned west.
                    Glanced at my stunned
            fingertips.

SIBLING RIVALRY

To be second born

in the nest of the skykillers.
God's terrible clarity.

CHICAGO

I came home late.
        She sat erect
                with her back to the lake.
    Arms folded around her knees.
                        Gazed out
        over her sprawling brood.
        Stared
                as if her eyes had
     just followed the sun
        down over the rim
                of the western neighborhoods.

When she saw me
        she pushed her dress
    down between her thighs.
                Patted the ground.
        Invited me to sit.
    I leaned my weight against her.
                And was again seduced.

PROGRESS

Years ago I had a small black and white TV.
                                        It was cute.
                Rabbit-ears.
                                No cable.
                        No VCR.
                                        No simulcast.
It weighed about six pounds
                        and sat on little
                plastic cube
                                over by the fireplace.
        I don't remember it ever being on.

The one I have now
                was turned on at the factory.
                                I can't remember
                it ever being off.

RAPTOR TRAP

A ball of radiating steel spikes atop a pole surrounding a bait.

Every time is the first time.
Every time is the last time.
Are there books
I should have read?
I'm impulsive.
But old enough to know better.
Know what better?
Is there a method?
Am I, like Stanislavski
"living truthfully
under imaginary circumstances?"
It's those Forties movies.
Ingrid Bergman and Charles Boyer
Black and white.
But here I come again.
High and right out of the sun.
Focused only on the target.
Plummeting earthward.
Picking up speed
every second.
Never seeing the danger.
Never seeing the danger.

MY LAST SEX POEM

I shall raise my sights.
        Think higher thoughts.
    Kant.
                Beethoven.
Refrain from daydream affairs
        with the girl at the other end
                of the counter.
Wish not to stroke
      those fine hairs
            that lie atop the small finger
      of her right hand.
And if the morning sunlight reveals
          through her white cotton blouse
     that the strap of her camisole has slipped
            from her left shoulder
 I will not stare transfixed
      at that delicate border of transparent lace
          slipping erotically
              down her breast.
Nor egg it on
        like a long-shot at the track
          pushing for the finish line.
These thoughts will be the farthest
          from my mind.
      Voltaire.
           Milton.
      Rabelais.

TWO HAIKU

Wabash and Lake

The el scratches its
                    finger across the
            blackboard.
Flashes cold
                    blue
            fire.

Wabash and Balbo

Whiskybeersticky
                    floors.
            GIRLS
            GIRLS
            GIRLS
                            Palidshirtsleeved
                    men.
        "Hi sugar."

ASCENT OF MAN

Lion 1:

"Their brain differentiates them from other animals."

Lion 2:

"True.

I always eat it first."

MALTA - APRIL 7, 1809

A boy about fifteen threw first.
            A small stone
        sailed past her shoulder and bounced
                    to the other side of the circle.
        One of the children threw next.
                            A game.
She stood in the center of the circle.
                    Her arms outstretched.
        Palms facing the crowd.
            A large brick
                    caught her square in the chest.
        A red rectangle bloomed
                        on her white shirt.
She staggered
        but her arms stretched out to the crowd.
                        Stones beat at her legs.
            A bat of limestone
                thrown by one of the men
                        snapped a rib.
        A smooth fieldstone exposed the bone
                over her left eye.
She dropped to her knees.
            Raised her arms over her head.
                        The circle closed tight.
                Her face pushed into her thighs.
        The rocks hurt less.
            A large woman with a dirty child
                        stepped forward.
                Crushed a full brick
                    into the girl's clotted hair.
Maria Calveccio
            who had fed two of Napoleon's soldiers
        died at nineteen.

WE

Scientists tell us
> we live under an ordinary star.
> Similar to billions of other suns.
>> With only random difference.

Viva la difference.

MATISSE'S CHAIR

Can we know anything
                    outside ourselves?
          Our time zone?
                    Can we hear Bach
                              after Steinway?
If we colorize Casablanca
                    can we cash in
                              our Double Indemnity?

What insight will allow us
                    to swim naked
                              in the Orinoco?
          Eat a monkey?

Should I compare it to a summer's day?
                              Or a cylinder?
                    Or a sonata?

Or look around what I know
                    and see Matisse's chair?

COMPANION

Her breast lies on my forearm.
                    Her small
          finger
                         rolled in my hand.
I push my brow
          up under
                    the blade of her shoulder.
Bury my nose
                    in the bed-smell
          of her tee-shirt.
Press my lips
                    secretly
                         against her back.

In the park
                    a car alarm
          whistles
                         unattended.

PRIORITIES

From a broken bowl
                        he drinks
             and does not see the long shadow
                            of the monkey-puzzle
        plot the motion of the universe.

MASHAIRI[1]

Dogo Bundi[2] rose early.
        Stroked the blade of his mkuki.[3]
      Brushed his kunoa[4] stone over the
               already sharp tip.
His children would eat meat today.
         His wife, Zuri Danzi[5]
      would again respect
           his power.
    The lion and the leopard
         would fear his footsteps.
Under the baobab
    dik-dik, and springbok
       grazed majani grass.
     Gnawed the bark of the rhigazum.

Kutia Mwindaja[6] also rose early.
         Three days of hunger
            and her cubs
   drove her from her den.
  Pushed her like the fish eagle's shadow
          over the kopje.

Dogo Bundi jogged low.
                    Held his lance close
                              to his thigh.
          Followed his spear through the elephant grass.

Kutia Mwindaja turned her ears to the soft footfalls
                    of Dogo Bundi.
          Slipped into the curtain
                              of grass.
Her cubs would eat meat today.
                    The San bushmen
          the Khoi and the Bakalanga
                    would fear her footsteps.

1 poem
2 small owl
3 lance
4 whetstone
5 beautiful dancer
6 shadow hunter

RESOLVE

I am tired from
                western culture.
        Maybe
                        culture in general.

I shall go and
                stand in the
        ocean
                        until all culture
                                runs out of me.
        Until all thinking and
                learning is
                        by capillary attraction
                                        and osmosis
                sucked from me.

I will sit close to a
                humming rock
                        remagnetize my brain
        rededicate my libido to
                                singularly pleasurable
                        endeavor.

CHEETAH

Dawn.
             The silhouette on the
       termite mound
                              yawns
                    a housecat yawn.
Considers the lioness
                         returning to the shade
             of the baobab tree.
Gives a workaday glance
                    to the gazelles on the
                              horizon.
Shakes off the dust
             and her cubs.
       Trots
                    to the starting
                              line.

UNCHANGED

Louis Pasteur slept with corpses.
                    Dressed in the bedclothes
          of the sick
                    and dead.
      "Malaria is not contagious."
          The anopheles mosquito
                    stands on its head
          to bite its victims.

Louis Patterson sleeps with corpses.
          Surrounded by Goethe
                         Rembrandt
               Beethoven.
          He will not stand on his head.
    He will skip class again today.
          When he awakens
               he will walk among
                         Nobelists.
      Nod to philosophers.
               Urinate beside architects.

Unchanged.

HER FACE

What burns the morning fog
                        its absence defining
                    the solitary night
        its aspect
                        the measure
            of a day?

FABLE

The people of Dagahabur
               Ethiopia in east Africa
       were starving.
The people in Washington
               District of Columbia
       eastern America
                  who were not starving
                      said
    "Let us send seeds
       so that these people
                 in Dagahabur
       may grow wheat and
         make bread."
The people in Dighton
               western Kansas
       "bread basket of the world"
                 who weren't starving
       either
but weren't eating nearly as well as the people
                 in Washington D.C.
       loaded tons and tons
               and tons
   of surplus wheat seeds
       onto big Hercules airplanes
        and flew them
to the people of Dagahabur
       who ate the seeds.
The people of Dagahabur
               Ethiopia in east Africa
       were starving.

HAIKU

Truth

        (invisible phantom)

                     eludes

                 envelops.

Water to the fish.

CRY OF THE CROCODILE

The crocodile
              chin on the muddy bank
          ponders infinity.
                          The regrets of misspent youth.
              Desire unfulfilled.
                                      Opportunity unanswered.
Stares appetent
                                          at the ocelot
          sleeping in a shaft of meridional sun.

SHE CAME TO PLAY

Micheline Ostermeyer
                    a slender
                        twenty-five-year-old pianist from Paris
                                stepped into the light.
            Chalked her anxious hands
                        her long fragile fingers.
Micheline Ostermeyer
                had wanted to be a concert pianist
            since she was four.
                            Now she stood before a crowd
                                    of thousands.
                Would she play Ravel?
                        Debussy?
No.
            She would throw the discus.
                Throw it farther than any woman
                                in the world
                        that summer day.
When she took her bow
                    they put olympic gold
                around her neck.
                                Her encore:
                    Gold in the shot-put.
        Curtain call:
                Bronze in the high-jump.
Micheline Ostermeyer
                            came to play.

THE WIND HAS CHANGED

He took her to a place beside a small lake.
                              "There is water here
                    we will immerse ourselves
                                        and the water
                          will not rise up against us."
                    He entreated her not to return
                                        to the Sea.
She was weary.
                         The shallow water felt warm.
          The water surrounded her
                                   and the Sun beat hard
                          upon her face.
The Moon unseen
                    rose in the sky.
          His words sat heavy in her mind.
                              And the Wind fell calm.

On the fifth day she returned
                    with him to their house on the hill.
          Sketchbook in hand
                              and wearing the yellow dress
                                        he bought her
                    at the place beside the small lake
                              she took the long path down
          to the beach.
"The Wind has changed.
                    The Sea will be calm.
          I will walk only on the breakwater.
                                        Stay dry."
Benign waves stroked foam and flotsam
                              across the damp sand.

118

She moved along the wall
        to the place where the breakwater
                met the jetty.
     The Wind was from the shore
          and the Sea was calm.
She carefully
      deliberately
            stepped stone to stone
        to the One Mile mark.

At the Two Mile mark she sat for a while
        faced back toward home and shore.
      Sketched the profile of a fisherman
              casting his line.
"I will walk out to the last rock.
       Keep my distance from the edge.
          Stay dry."

She stood and watched
       the Red Number-Two sea buoy
     rise and pitch with the ocean rollers.
           Again turned her gaze
       homeward
     with the toll of the bell buoy.
Suddenly, the Sea swept up.
         Pushed over her ankles.
      Rushed up her thighs.
          Lifted her yellow dress.
She held her left arm outstretched
       defiant against the Sea.
   Her eyes burned.
         Brine filled her nostrils.

Again the Sea rose up around her.
                    Spoke to her.
          "You will not return to the man
                    and the house on the hill."
          Now the Sea was warm
                    as it rushed between her thighs.
          Over her breasts.
                              She raised her arms.
          The Sea took her book
                    and the yellow dress.

Standing naked on the last stone
                    she turned again homeward.
          Fell into the Sea.

O.R. 6

For Dr. Verna Baughman anesthesiologist.

When the hour came
                    with its knives and needles
            and I lay trapped
                        in the madness
                            of that room
        an angel
                    beautiful
            radiant
                                green
        lifted my land to her breast
                    spread her wings over me.

THE OLD LION

For Josephine.

There is a green card table.
                              Folding chair.
       A bald place
              out beyond the house
                      where Richard sat.
The meercats had been documented.
                    Filmed.
           Tagged.
       Grant money spent.
                  Sixteen years in the Mara Valley.
From his chair
          Richard stared over the dry grass.
               A hundred yards out
          an old lion stared back.
      He had come after the last rains.
                Driven out of his pride
       by younger rivals.
Sara stood at the sink.
              Scrubbed the breakfast frypan.
     Looked hopelessly out at her husband.
       Would they take their daughter
                 back to England?
        Back to Michigan?
Richard took his 32 Smith & Wesson
            from its holster.
      Could not recall the last time
               he had fired it.
        Never killed anything.
     He rotated the cylinder in his hand.
            Four live rounds.
       Two spent casings.

He slipped the pistol back
into its holster.
Walked toward the old lion.
It would be quick, he thought.
Fitting.
ZOOLOGIST KILLED BY LION.
He approached the old lion.
It stood
puzzled.
Retreated.
He pushed on.
Again the lion retreated.
Richard's last fantasy
played out.
He turned.
Looked back at his house.
He thought he could see Sara
at the kitchen sink.
The pistol's report sent a quiver
through the lion.
Richard slumped into the dead grass.

There is a bald place
out past the house
where an old lion sleeps.

THE BRASS RING

I started life
            riding the one fixed
      to the platform.
                        Soon
            I climbed up on a leaping back
      with a golden pole.
                  Reared head.
                              Wild eye.
                  Gaping mouth.
      I leaned out.
                  Reached for the ring.

Now friends I don't know
            stand in a chilly circle around me.
      And in another field
                  a horse beckons
      with live breath.
                        Turns and runs.

FRANCINE READS HER POEM

The wind arrow starts a deliberate turn to the
                                    North East.
                    The top of the main
                              fills.
My pencil escapes.
              Rolls across a chart.
        I rush to the cockpit.
                                    Take the wheel
                    as the boom snaps leeward.
The ship heels.
              Drives forward.
        I sheet in the jib.
                    Trim the main.
The toerail dives toward quickly forming
                                    whitecaps.
              Spray kicks over the windward deck.
I catch my reflection
                    in the dome of the binnacle compass.
"We're in for a ride."

ROADKILL

From the bedroom my wife's voice pried
           through the chaos of the TV news.
      I pressed mute.
                The action amplified.
                    And again I saw her
          pounding on the window glass.

She had seemed small
         like the car
             in the circle of fire.
      The grass, the brush, the highway itself
                        in flame.
One fire-fighter
        wild
             ran toward the car.
The woman
     like a bird in a trap
              beat against each pane.
         Screamed mute for escape.
                        Rescue.
An axe
        smashed
             through the streetside window.
     There was only her scream
             and the fire.

The orange gloves of the fireman
                              lost in the flame
                      dragged her
                                     over the sill
            through the charred grass
                   to a clearing beside the highway.
A patrolman flagged my car around the last
                              emergency vehicle.
                  The screaming
                                  stopped.

I pressed the mute button.
          On. Off. On. Off. On. Off.

THE VALUE OF HISTORY

A man kills a man
          for stealing his pig.
     Understandable.

A man kills a man
        who looks like
              the kind of a man
          who might
    steal his pig.

History.

FOUR HAIKU

Helplessly I watch
         as the stern light fades from view.
     Overboard alone.

My sleeping crew deaf
         blind to my hapless plight.
     Undisturbed sail on.

Cold overwhelms fear.
         I resign myself to sleep.
     Sleep resigns to death.

I who loved her
         loved her icy waves and spray
     am taken to her.

STEPPING IN AN ANTHILL

Or misunderstanding one's lover.

First the soldiers scramble up.
Mandibles agape.
Armed.
Combat prescient.
Then the workers.
(Damage repair.)
Pebbles removed.
Cavities filled.
Passageways cleared.
Above the rebuilding
extravagate soldiers maintain guard.
Rim the hill.
Bite out at remnant danger.
Soon the workers recure the mound.
Formic messages signal "all clear."
Thwarted soldiers
execute a final sweep of the perimeter.
Disappear.

HERO'S CHILD

Quickly
                    straight
          and tall
                                        a seedling grows.
Dies
          in shadow of the tree.

REFUGE

Paint your house crimson.
                    Cerulean blue.
          Stand on the promontory in that sulphur dress.
Even if you don't see me
                    at first.
          Wave to the horizon.
     Bring me in.

ERECHTHEUM THEATRE

How long will they wait?
The six of them.
They've waited so long.
And for what?
And for whom?
Friends who said they needed them?
Husbands who didn't?
Children who grew up anyway?
But it's not like they've been doing
nothing.
They've been holding up that little theatre
and doing a damn good job.
I mean it's not like
they've been doing
nothing.
I'll bet they were beautiful
before time and the wind
wore away their smiles
and their dreams.

PERSONAL BEST

We hear nothing.
        They hear the private
                    silent
               starting gun.
     The gazelle.
        The cheetah.
We see a brief race
        ending in
            death.
                    The swift.
              The swiftest.
They run a never ending relay.
           The gazelle.
       The cheetah.
            Handing off
              swiftness
        to their own kind.

NEGRO ATTACKED BY A LEOPARD

After a painting by Henry Rousseau.

There are
          panthers
                              in the Paris Conservatory.
                    Rousseau had seen them
                                                  in Merida.
                              Brought them home
                    in his head.
Pictured them behind
                    the banana flowers.
                                        Painted them beneath
                              the Heliconias of the
          Paris Conservatory.

IMMORTALITY

My girlfriend paints portraits.
                              Life-size.
                    Full-figure.
Last year she painted me.
                         Said I seemed
                                        smaller
                              on canvas.
We checked the measurements.
                            I remain:
                                 73 inches.
          My image:
               70 inches.

Not even my lover wants
                         all
               of me.

POLICE PHOTO

A solitary
                    empty
          black leather
                              wingtip
               with the laces tied
                         sits picturesque beside
          the slender
                    rectangular leg
               of a small
                              white lacquered
                                        table.
The neck of a Bordeaux bottle
               and the silver handle of a
                         fork
          extend over the edge of
                    an out-of-view
                              tabletop.
Splatter stains of blood
               obscure the "f i n o"
                         in a Portofino poster.
                    Trail down the wall
          to the face
                    of what used to be
                              Lenny Fontana.
          A black river frames his head
               and extends to his stocking foot.
A scene outside of space and time.
                    Surrounded by police tape.
          Reminding us not to crossover.
                              Not to step outside.

ORDER

Professor Foxworthy plugs numbers
               into his formulae.
     $X = X$
        The world falls into place.
             Effort versus reward.
     Safety versus danger.
        The needle centers.

A hyena howls in the amber dusk.
        The leopard feels the bump
             and nudge
       of cubs at her side.
     $X = X$

Joyce Foxworthy sits on the edge
           of her bed.
        Pulls buttons off her DKNY blouse.
     Stares at the closet latch.
        Division by zero.
          The computer locks.
     $X < X$
        The needle drifts.

The hyena cubs lumber back
          into the den.
        The world falls into place.

Mother of pearl buttons
           reflect on the floor.

The leopard watches the birth
           of a Thompson's Gazelle.
      The needle centers.

Professor Foxworthy pushes back
           in his chair.
   $X = X$
           Drops his number six Eberhard Faber
           into a Goofy cup.

Mascara stains the DKNY blouse.

LONGING

The Sargent Major*

                         thrown upon the shore
           gapes
              hypoxic.
I wait for the wave
                your return
       that will sweep me
  back
                  into the sea.

*a small reef fish

140

NADJA SALERNO SONNENBERG

I sat in the second row
         second seat from the aisle.
                      She stood at the edge
                of the stage
         feet shoulder-width apart.
             A shortstop waiting for a hard
                              grounder.
                      But more like the bridge
                of the violin.
         Her body squeezed
                between the strings
                         and the wooden stage.
She lifted the instrument
                to her shoulder.
             Laid her cheek down upon the violin.
         Raised the bow to the strings.
                      Bit her lip.
                Leapt into a place that we
                              will never know.
When all the blood
                had run out of her
         and into the hungry soul
                      of the composer
             she opened her eyes.
                              Smiled.
                Let down the violin.

THE END OF BEAUTY

Sometimes Nature kills its children.
                                Eats. Freezes. Burns.
              Hurls them
                  broken
        to the forest floor.
                                    We cry to God.
The indomitable crocodile
                    returns to her nest.
              Finds the mongoose
                      slurping down
        the last of her brood.
                                Beautifully.
                    Perfectly.
              And the serval cat
                      dines
                on new-born mongoose.
Two houses down the block
                  Charlie Wilson
        pushes little Lydia Thompson
                        into his car.
                  Rapes her.
              Kills her.
            Packs her into an oil drum.
                                We cry to God.
We cry for Lydia Thompson.
        We cry for Charlie Wilson.

The young male lion

                  enters the pride.
          Takes each cub in his jaws.

                      Snaps its spine.
            Beautifully.

                Perfectly.

And the mongoose

        who's name is AIDS or EBOLA
      scampers through the nursery.

                     We cry to God
          for the end of beauty.

BACK AND FORTH

"There's a nest in the boom."
      Stephanie pointed from the cockpit
                              and I
                      reaching in
        expecting to rake out
           just another mess to clean up
    felt heat and carefully pulled out
      the painstakingly perfectly
           wellmeaningly constructed nest
with its four naked
      just-hatched inhabitants.
I lowered them so Stephanie could see.
    "Put them back.
           Quickly.
              Put them back."

Can only God save us?
      Don't we get it?
    Forth is what we do.
             Forth we have down.
          Forth we do with a vengeance.
The man on TV said we can't put the oil back
               into the tanker.
      And the shrimp will not
           come back to the estuary.
I believe him.
      These birds will never fly.
        Trees will not grow back
    in the rainforest.

Not yet being gods we can only go forth.
We are limited to that.
We have to do it right the first time.
The birds failed.
They had to be out of that boom by June 12.
Or die.
In another universe
a couple of days either way.
Maybe.

"Can't we save them?"
The question angered me.
Are the Israelis going to invite the Palestinians
back to Jerusalem?
Shall we give Florida back to Osceola?
Was I going to save the birds?

I stood there really wanting to put them back
but in a representative gesture
of my species
I set them aside in a cool place.
To die of course.
And went forth to what I was doing.

RED SHIFT

Because
                    the universe is expanding.
                                Because the universe
            is collapsing in on itself.
                                Because the universe
                is at times
                            totally out of my
                                    personal control.
A small
            but very bright
                            star
                soon will move northward.
                                Her red-shift taillights
                    will drop below the
                                    horizon
            out of reach
                    of my forty-second parallel
                                north-side Chicago
                    eyes.
And surely
                on some black sea
                            one black night
                I'll look to the stars
                                for direction.

Rigel will smile reassuringly
                  from the left foot
        of Orion.
                        Spica will remain
                faithful in Virgo.
But the girl who answers the phone
        in the second floor reading room
                of the
            Newberry Library
                      won't be
    Josephine.

OVERBOARD

Tonight it is not the shark
                        nor the sea serpent
                                    that I fear.
            But an aloneness
                    heavier than the horizonless sky.
An isolation pressing me
                        again and again
                                    under
                        the surface of the sea.
My leaden boots
        are the monsters of the deep.
                        My slicker the serpent
                entangling every limb.
No longer ago
        than the telling of this
                    I was safe.
                Laughing at the storm.
                        Scoffing the mounting waves.
When the scorned fury of the sea
                reached up and swept me from
        light and warmth.
                        Circled crosses on a chart.
So this unplotted way-point
                is my final destination.
        These storm petrels
                    my last reception.
All that was safe
                has slipped into the darkness
        of distance.
                        As I will soon slip
                                    into a darkness.
                Deeper even than the sea.

NOVA SCOTIA - SOUTHEASTERN COAST

I get lost in maps.
                    I'll unfold one
          onto the dining room
                              table.
          Press it out flat
                    with the palm of my
                                        hand.
Bring the lamp down close.
                         Adjust my reading glasses.
               Isolate myself on
     Nova Scotia - Southeastern Coast.
I slide my fingers over
               faint pencil lines.
          Feel my way down the coast:
                              Brazil Rock.
                    Cape Sable.
          The shallows and wrecks off Tusket
                    Island.
"You wanna clear the table, we'll have dinner."

Yarmouth.
          The Bay of Fundy.

ONLY THE FEMALES BITE

A friend's boy of eleven asked
                "Are you afraid of snakes?"
                                "No," I replied.
        "Are you afraid of lions?"
                                I told him of the time
                        I was in the leopard's cage.
"I guess you're not afraid of anything."
                "No, I'm just not afraid of
the things you're afraid of."

His mother
                like most
                                had spent years
        pointing out things to fear.
                                All the dangers
                he might encounter.
        All the things that might hurt him.

My mother
                spent a great deal of time
                        pointing out things not to fear.
        "This won't hurt you," she'd say.
                        And we'd turn over logs
        until we found a snake.
Or we'd climb to the top of a tree
                        or up a smokestack ladder.
                "Don't look down.
        The top rung is as safe as the bottom one."

As a child I faced a world of few fears.
                    The exception was women.
          I was effectively warned of their myriad
                              and absolute dangers.
The first was Mary Lane.
               "You two weren't taking off
                    your clothes or anything?"
          I supposed that if I saw Mary Lane
                                   naked
               I'd turn into a stag like Actaeon.
Later I was warned about Sandra.
          "She's the kind of girl that will get pregnant
                              very easily."

So at forty-eight
               three days and five hundred miles
          out of Bermuda
                         lashed to the backstay
                    facing seventy knot winds
               sixty foot waves
                         the only thing I feared
          the only thing I was not prepared for
               was the frightened five-foot-four
                                        woman
                         below deck
               trying to cook a little dinner
                         on a gimbaled stove.

THE UNSPEAKABLE YEARS

Hey, the Fifties.
                    My fifty-five Ford Fairlane
                                   convertible.
                    (should've kept that car)
          The Platters.
                              Sandra.
And the Sixties.
                    Ed Sullivan.
          The Beetles.
                                   Free love.
                    (should've kept that car)
The Seventies.
                    Paisleys.
                                   Elephant bells.
The Eighties and The Nineties.
                         But now...
The Millennium.
          2000.
          The double zero decade.
                         Unspeakable years.
          O – one through o – nine.
               "Back in aught six..."
                              Followed by
                         unintelligible teens.
          Then, finally...
Hey, the Twenties.

LOVE

If you roll love
           over
                      onto its back.
          Pull it out of its warm
                      dark
                            hole.
              Place it on the dappled
                      sunlit side of
                              a tree.
Its chrysalis will often
              recreate itself
                  into veilless
    art.

NIGHT TRAIN

A black pig dead
          lies in Union Station.
     I am fighting sleep.
               Red-blood-black-white
         chessboard floats me dizzy
and columns wait for players
        left the game.
Dead it moves.
         A ruby slit drawn
               throat to belly births
           bloodslick rats.
     One then a hundred
        pass from her stomach.
               Huddle in the shadow
        of the column.
Rubbing my eyes
        I adjust the pain
             of my shoulderstrap.
        Outstretch my arm.
     Set a course around the column.
        Feel it rotate cool under my fingers.
Dead pig and checkerboard disappear.
           Cold marble feels now
        veined leather warm.
     Bat's wing metamorphosed rats
             cling to the shadow
        of the column.
Fearing further plot development
              I take bishop's path
      to sidewalk sunlight's
wakefulness.

DILEMMA

Should I send her
                 one of my poems?
                                   Or stay
                      in the comic strip?
Polish the blazer buttons?
               Or reveal that
                   parcel of vain strivings?
Bad poetry is well dug-in
               retreat impossible.
                         Bad sex is inevitable
                 but improves
                           with reading.
Stay in the comic strip
              or turn the page?
         Zap! Wow! Yipes!

LOOKING FOR THE SCORECARD

I'm thinking I should have this framed.
                              Hung on the wall
                 in the living room.
                              My first published poem.
                                        Next to
          BEST NEWSPAPER AD 1974.
                    Or this picture of me and Cousteau.
                                   in our wet-suits.
Impress somebody.
          No
                         here's one of me hot-dogging
                              down the slopes in Aspen.
                    Wait
          here I am playing the violin for
                              spelunking in
                                   flying my plane over
                    sailing through…

I am that china-shop bull.
                    Bumping into just about everything.
          Catching it just before it smashes.
                                        Polishing it off.
                    Putting it back on the table.
Running into the next room.
                         A smiley-faced guy
                    wanting to have a good day
                                   everyday.

There are some other pictures in this box.
People I didn't catch.
People who rolled under the table.
Broken a little.
Every now and then one will roll out.
Turn its blemish from me.
Ask how'm I doing.
If I'm still...

I'm not.
But I'm always glad to see them.
"Have you seen that trick I do with the penny?
I could fly down to Atlanta..."

"JUST BECAUSE I LET YOU FUCK ME."

BJ's story.

Sara is naked.
                    Her Jack Daniels makes reckless
        slushy ellipses as she holds court
                                on the back
                of my hunter green couch.
Eddie Appleton and Tony Fratelli
                    are licking their visual plates
                                clean.
                    I hate their
                                        staying.
        Sitting there
                drinking in the impromptu show.
In the kitchen door I wait.
                        Blurred with anger.
                    Frozen.
                                Impotent.
"B.J., some more Jack."
                Her glass orbits in my direction.
        I step forward.
                        Fill her glass.
                She baits me to scold her nakedness.
I retreat to the kitchen
            trying to ignore the indelible movie
                        playing out in the next room.
                Finally,
        satisfied with my humiliation
                        she steps off the couch.
                Disappears into the bedroom.

GDS 301 GRAPHIC DESIGN

Feral dogs are lapping at my feet.
            The pool of my dissolving body
                        spreads
      over the white marred linoleum.
                  Behind me the blackboard rises.
            Jason, in the second row
                  looks up from his notes.
      Kandinsky and Miro
                        slosh
                              liquesce
            in my brain.
Now the pack is eight.
                  Maybe ten.
            Lapping me up.
                  A girl in the back of the class
      (I don't know her name.)
                        raises her hand.
      "I have to leave
                        early
                  Mr. Pitts."
I flow under
            around her unlaced Reeboks.
      The dogs clatter around the slick floor.
                  Nose under each desk.
            Jason doodles super heroes
      in the margin of his notebook.
                  The floor is dry.

OUTTA CONTROL

It's the middle of the night.
                    The wind has piped up.
            I'm running.
                              Dead down.
                    With the chute.
"I should have dumped the thing
                    when I could."
The speed-o is
            nine
                              up the backs.
                    Pegged
                              down the faces.
I'll pitch-pole if it gets any worse.
                    And it's blowing stink.
      If I turn starboard
                              I'll pick up speed.
                    Round-up.
                              Or roll.
            Port.
                    No better.
I'm gonna ride it out.

THE NEXT WOMAN I MEET

The first woman I met
              lifted me to her breast
        stuck it in my mouth
           and told me
    (in so many words)
        that all things good and wonderful
           flowed from it.
This first woman also told me
           how beautiful
             wonderful
      and smart
                I was.
    How life would be one great adventure
           with me at the helm.

The second woman I met
           didn't want her breast
            in my mouth.
      Thought I was less than wonderful
             for asking.
    Told me
      (in so many words)
      I was a little overweight.
           There was a thin spot
on the back of my head.
        And my adventure
             was to conquer
      bigger paychecks.
         Additional bedrooms.

JUST PART OF THE NIGHT

I was early.
        But then I'm always early.
                        It's hard to be late
                when you're meeting someone
                        at eleven o'clock in the evening.
                And a beautiful Chicago evening it was.
So I strolled my tux and I
                down by the river
                through that little park
                        above Rush and Hubbard.
Well, I was walking along
                (you know me)
                        hands behind my back
                head looking up at
                        Ursa Major
                humming one of my
                        made-up-on-the-spot
                        Russian folktunes
                                when
"Hey, wait a minute," there she was
                her left arm around my shoulder
        her right hand slipped, "Zowee"
                right down inside the front
        of my pants.
The Russians picked up the beat.
                And the pitch.
        "You sure are dressed up fit to kill, Honey."
                "You're rather decked out yourself"
                                I said.

"You want some of what I've got?" she asked.
                              I thought to myself
              Yes, I would like my balls back.
                    But I said, "No, not tonight."
She tightened her grip on my private parts.
                              "You ain't gay are you
              Honey?"
Again, I answered in the negative.
                    "You ain't got nothing against
        black women have you?"
                              We walked a block
                    and as we approached the edge
                                        of the park
        she gave me a final squeeze.
"Catch you later, Honey."
                    She wheeled around
                              and as I watched
        walked back into the park.
I smiled
        checked my watch
                    looked up to see if the Dipper
              was still there.
Walked down to Shaw's
                              still early.

HYDRA

NOVEMBER RAIN

It sounds like rain again.
                    That soft rhythmic spatter.
          Gentle drops upon a wooden sill.
But it isn't rain.
                    It's the donkey man.
                              His eternal Doric train.
               Its dateless pace
against the smooth cobblestones.
"Brrrttt, brrrttt, nea, brrrttt."
                         I push up on my elbow.
          Shake clouds and webs
                              from my brain.
     Catch a cobalt stroke of Mediterranean.
Fall back into the serene provocation
                         of Hydra.

COMING HOME

A short blast of the horn.
                    I looked up from my writing.
            The Saronicos ferry slipped into port.
                              Eleven-forty a.m.
The café where I nurse my filtered coffee
                sits just in front of the church
                              bell tower.
The tower answered the ship.
                    One bell.
Then I saw them.
            A young boy in gold brocade
                carrying a larger-than-himself cross
                              stepped from the boat.
Six pallbearers.
                Stern faces and dark suits
                              followed.
A small group of women
                    seven or eight
                              all in black
            all carrying small bits of luggage
                    pressed toward the church.
A younger woman
            Nike travel bag over her shoulder
            a small package of Kleenex
                              in her right hand
                walked close to the coffin.
As she passed my table she smiled politely.
            I returned the expression.
        The momentary congruence
                    brought back her tears.
        She turned with the others
                              into the church.

PASSAGE

Lovers have departed the island.
            Couples that drank at each other's loins
      licked their fingers
         and left.
Impotent friends remain.
       Share a touch.
            An innuendo.
       A filtered coffee.
She looks up from her sketchbook.
    "We should pick up basil
           before the market closes."
I smile.
       Ask the progress of her drawings.
            Try to write.
    Face my insatiate longing.

HYDRIAN ALCHEMY

The first nail came out
                    long and straight.
          Decades ago
              the wound had healed.
                              The nail hung loose
                    in its carapace.
My trail had taken me
                to an ancient gate.
                          The rails weathered hard.
            Goats restrained by the enclosure
                  witnessed mute my thievery.
The second nail
          took more effort
                                  its shank twisted
                    by rings in the post.
This fence would not miss
                        these fasteners.
          Long ago reinforced
                  by newer
                                  machine-made.
The third nail
          as the first
                slipped out of its cavity
                          with a gentle tug
                  of my thumb and forefinger.

A hundred years ago
    a smith had forged these spikes.
   Pounded their shape
     in the dies of his anvil.
   For decades they bound
       wood to wood.
   Now I roll them over in my hand.
Each uniquely transfigured:
   An extinct tiger's canine.
      A serpent's rib.
   A witch's hatpin.
Together:
   Nordic runes.
     Hebrew calligraphy.
   Celtic talismans.

MICHAEL LAWRENCE
For the painter/sculptor on the occasion of his fifty-eighth birthday.

He pours hot
        wax
              on the marble top of his
                        dresser.
Birds
      disguised as women's hats
              (phoenixes)
                    arise
              chased by
    ebullient not-so-chaste
          maidens.
Lubricious gentlemen
        doves in hand
              penises erect
    step out of blue paintings.
A Ferlinghetti naked nude
        having borrowed Chagall's
             horse
    dismounts and tangos
      with a Parisian bon vivant.
The sculptor
    Einstein's hair
      Cagney's twinkle
        waves his magic baton
  delighted in his
    joyous conception.

REASONS TO LIVE IN HYDRA: #17

You know that sound a motorcycle makes
                                            when it revs up
                    to about three thousand rpm
                                            just before it shifts into third?
No.

VLICHOS ON HYDRA

Most of the beach umbrellas
                    had been taken in.
        Of the ones left
                only four or five had their thatched
                                    tops.
It was late October.
            The taverna had closed.
        The beach resort
                    had pulled up stakes in
                                September.
A stringy young man
            of about thirty
                    stood calf-deep in the sea.
        Watched a small boy's head and arms
                        splash a few metres out.
The woman lay spread eagle
            on an orange-striped beach towel.
        A child in a blue two-piece
                    bathing suit
            played in the sand next to the blanket.
They weren't Greek.
                Maybe English
                            or Scandinavian.
The water taxi had deposited them
                    on the small jetty.
Their suitcases
            and street clothes
        were neatly arranged
                in the shade of
                        one umbrella.

How out-of-place
        they seemed.
                How in-place
                    they were.
It was as if everybody was there
                  around them.
      The music from the taverna
                    loudly playing.
Waiters and bus-boys
        pouring ouzo.
                  Delivering mezedes.
            Clearing tables.
The young boy turned in the water.
                      Shouted.
            Waved to his mother.
      She raised up on her elbow.
                "Geh nicht so weit."
        Gazed over at her husband.
                Relaxed back
            into the sand.

WINTER'S TOLL

Cats are dying on Hydra.
                    It's December.
          The kittens of spring
                         that plied each tourist
                    every transient expatriate
       for scraps of charity
                won't see summer.
Wild harbor cats that beg
                          a red mullet or a herring
                    from the fishermen
                              have a chance.
          When the boats come out of the water
                    they'll make do
               with garbage.
                                   Mice.
Restaurant and town cats
                     used to handouts will starve.
          Or be poisoned by the locals.
April will bring
          tourists with their table droppings.
                    Expatriates with their visas
               and sardines.
Kittens.

FISH AND WINE

I stand naked at the bathroom sink
                                brushing my teeth.
            Towel damp out of the shower
                        she sits spreadlegged on the toilet.
I stare at the small tract of curls
                        between her thighs.
She says we shouldn't have sex for awhile.
                                Need to work things out.
            "We should pick up some fish
                        and maybe a bottle of wine
            when we walk into port."
I nod.
            I will be fun to cook fish.
                                Drink wine.